Collage

Sue Stocks

With photographs by Chris Fairclough

Thomson Learning • New York

FIRST ARTS & CRAFTS

Books in this series

Collage
Drawing
Painting
Printing

First published in the
United States in 1994 by
Thomson Learning
115 Fifth Avenue
New York, NY 10003

First published in Great Britain in 1994 by Wayland (Publishers) Ltd.

Library of Congress Cataloging-in-Publication Data
Stocks, Sue.
Collage / Sue Stocks ; with photographs by Chris Fairclough.
p.   cm. — (First arts & crafts)
Includes bibliographical references and index.
ISBN 1-56847-161-0
1. Collage — Juvenile literature. [1. Collage. 2. Handicraft.]
I. Fairclough, Chris, ill. II. Title. III. Series.
TT910.S77   1994
702'.8'12—dc20   93-46891

Printed in Italy

Contents

What is collage?

Collage is the art of gluing different materials onto a background to make a picture. You can make collages with just about anything. Look around and see what you can find. This collage is made from shapes cut out of painted paper.

Here are some ideas for things you can use to make a collage – scraps of fabric, shells, beads, dried seeds and pods, bottle caps, wood shavings and sawdust, different papers, corrugated cardboard, leaves and grasses, dried pasta and lentils, candy wrappers, aluminum foil, and crushed, rinsed eggshells.
Collect as many items as you wish and put them in a cardboard box.

You will need:

A cardboard box

Scissors

Glue

Different materials for making your collages

This can be your collage box. Use it to store the materials you collect to make your collages. Keep adding to your box as you find new things to use. You can decorate your box by sticking some of the things onto it.

Making a collage

You can make a collage out of one material or many different materials. You can make big collages or small ones. Small ones can be made with seeds, beads, and thread.

You will need:
Your collage box
Scissors
Glue
Cardboard
Paper

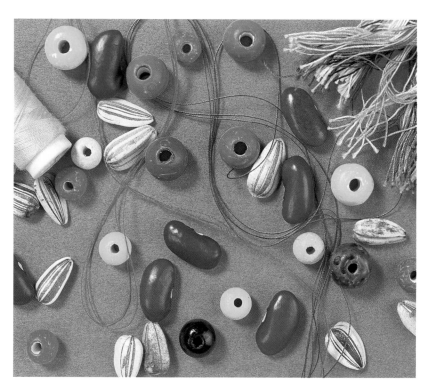

You can cut or tear paper into different sized pieces. Torn paper has interesting edges. You can scrunch it up into different shapes or overlap the pieces as you glue them down.

When you make a collage it is usually best to put in the background first. This can be done by sticking large pieces of paper or fabric over a cardboard base before you add the smaller materials.

- Cut some pieces of cardboard about six inches square.
- Choose some materials from your box and practice making patterns by gluing them onto the squares. You will need to put glue on your cardboard each time you add something.
- Sprinkle some sand onto one of the squares. When it is dry, glue on some wood shavings.
- Try gluing seeds, dried pasta, fabric, or torn paper onto other squares.

Come up with your own ideas. Collect your squares and glue them onto a big sheet of colored cardboard.

Windows

Windows come in different shapes and sizes. You see many interesting things when you look through windows. Look at this collage of a toy shop. It is more than six feet wide.

The Toy Shop by Peter Blake (b.1932).

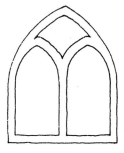 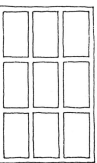  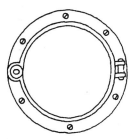 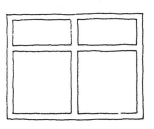

You can make your own collage of a view through a window. You might be looking out of the window or looking in. If you look out you might see houses, countryside, sky, or the sea. What else might you see through a window? What would you see if you looked in through a window?

There are windows in cottages and castles, cars and airplanes. Can you think of other windows? Choose your favorite window to make a collage.

You will need:

Your collage box

Scissors

Glue

Stiff cardboard

Cardboard

Use as many different materials as you can.

- Make the background first.
- Build up your picture by gluing down materials from your collage box.
- Cut a window frame from cardboard and glue it on top of your collage.

When you have finished your picture, hang it on the wall. Next time, make another window with a different view.

Faces

Look at this painting called *Spring*. The artist is famous for strange pictures like this. What do you think of it?

You will need:

Old magazines

Scissors

Glue

Paper

Pencil

Spring by Giuseppe Arcimboldo (1527-1593).

- Cut out an assortment of eyes, noses, mouths, eyebrows, and ears from pictures in old magazines.
- Make a pile of each.
- Cut out pictures that include different skin colors.
- Make a pile of each.
- Do the same with different hair colors.

Now you are ready to make a funny face.

- Draw the outline of a head on your sheet of paper. Make it big, and do not draw in the eyes, nose, or mouth.
- Use pieces from your pile of skin colors to make the background of the face.
- Tear the pieces of paper and overlap them when you glue them down.
- Glue on eyes, eyebrows, ears, and a mouth. Choose a big nose!
- Tear or cut paper for the hair and glue it on.

Next time, make a different face. Make a row of funny faces. Which do you like best?

Stained-glass windows

Look at the pictures of stained-glass windows below. Look at all the colors. When light shines through stained-glass windows, the colors are brighter. Have you seen any windows like these?

Sometimes stained-glass windows tell a story or make a picture. Sometimes they just make a pattern. The window below on the right was made for a synagogue in Jerusalem, Israel. The picture on the left is the painting from which a window was copied for the new Tate Gallery in St. Ives, Cornwall, in England.

Design for Big Window - Tate Gallery St. Ives: April 1992 (Gouache: 185 x 165mm) by Patrick Heron (b.1920).

The Tribe of Benjamin from the series *The Twelve Tribes of Israel* by Marc Chagall (1887-1985).

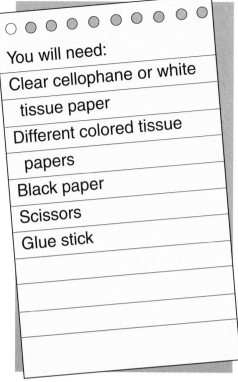

You will need:

Clear cellophane or white tissue paper

Different colored tissue papers

Black paper

Scissors

Glue stick

- Cut some thin strips of black paper.
- Use them to make a window frame.
- Glue the clear cellophane or white tissue paper onto the window frame. You should now have a window.
- Tear and cut large and small pieces of colored tissue paper.
- Stick these pieces onto the window. Try overlapping some of them.

Now turn your collage over so that all the glue is on the back. Hold your collage up to the light. Look at the beautiful, bright colors. See how the colors change where they overlap. You can lay thin strips of black paper over your window to make a different pattern. Tape your finished picture to a window.

Bird's-eye view

Pretend you are a bird, or a pilot in a plane, flying over the countryside. Look down at the ground. What colors would you see? Greens, yellows, and browns perhaps.

Think of the patterns in fields that have just been plowed. Grass and corn grow in fields. Think of all the different textures, shapes, and colors of the fields.

Look at this photograph taken from the air. Does it remind you of anything?

- Collect a variety of country colors from the pages of old magazines.
- Make separate piles of the different colors.
- Draw your bird's-eye view of the landscape on the cardboard. Draw only the shapes of the fields.
- Tear your colored paper and magazine pictures into different shapes and sizes, like the fields in the photograph.
- Glue them next to each other.
- Now you can glue down thin strips as hedges. See the patterns they make.

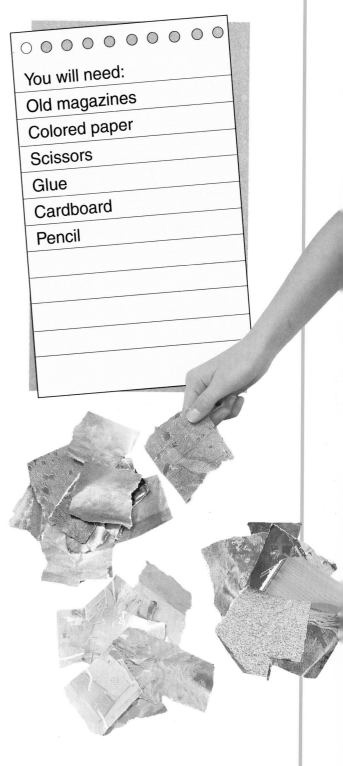

You will need:
Old magazines
Colored paper
Scissors
Glue
Cardboard
Pencil

You could paint a picture of a flying bird. Make it big and glue it onto the landscape. When you have finished your collage, hang it on the wall.

Clowns

Look at these pictures of colorful clowns. Do you think they have funny faces?

Draw a picture of a different clown. What color will the nose be? Will the hair be curly?

Make a collage of a clown. Look in your collage box for things you can use to make the face. You could use wood shavings or dried spaghetti for the clown's hair, bottle caps for the eyes, and sunflower seeds for the teeth.

- Cut out a piece of paper or fabric in the shape of the clown's face. Make it big. Don't forget the ears!
- Glue the face onto the cardboard.
- Glue down all the other things you have chosen to make the face. Make your collage colorful.

When you have finished, think of a name for your clown. You could also make a collage of the Big Top, or the circus ring with lots of clowns.

Wild animals

Think of some animals with interesting markings on their coats, such as leopards, tigers, and snakes. What other animals can you think of?

Now think of some black-and-white animals, such as pandas. Can you think of some more? Now find some black-and-white pictures of wild animals.

Collect a variety of black-and-white materials to make a collage of an animal with interesting markings.

You will need:

Black and white papers,
including newspaper

Black and white fabrics

Any other black and white
things from your collage
box

Scissors

Glue

Cardboard

Pencil

- Draw the outline of your animal on the cardboard. Make it big.
- Put in the background first. Will there be trees in your picture?
- Now make your animal. Tear and cut the papers and fabrics to make the shapes you want.

Next time, make a different animal with colored materials. You could make a very big, colorful collage of Noah's Ark. Ask a friend to help you.

Under water

This picture was made by turning paper into pulp and pressing it into molds. The artist made twenty-nine pictures like this and called them *Paper Pools*.

Le Plongeur (Paper Pool 18) 1978 72 x 171" by David Hockney (b.1937).

Look at any pictures or books you have about water, swimming pools, the sea, ponds, lakes, and rivers. Look at the colors in the water.

Now look at this photograph of a brightly colored fish.

Collect anything you can think of that would make an interesting collage of some fish.

- Tear your colored tissue into different shapes.
- Overlap the shapes as you glue them onto a very big piece of cardboard to make a water collage.
- Make a collage of a fish on another piece of paper. Use beads, sequins, and scraps of fabric or foil to show its scales. Use bright colors.
- Cut out your fish and glue it onto your water collage.
- Make some more fish, big ones and small ones. Glue these down too.
- Use some more torn tissue to glue over parts of the fish. See how they change color.

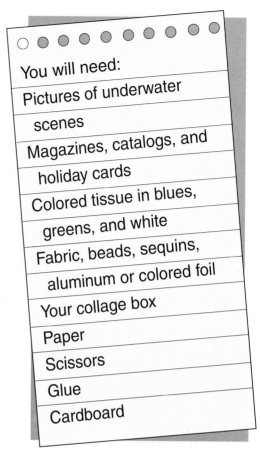

You will need:

Pictures of underwater scenes

Magazines, catalogs, and holiday cards

Colored tissue in blues, greens, and white

Fabric, beads, sequins, aluminum or colored foil

Your collage box

Paper

Scissors

Glue

Cardboard

Rain forests

Think about all the different colors you would find in a rain forest. Would there be many different greens? How big would the plants and trees be?

Look at this painting called *Exotic Landscape.* It could have been a collage.

Exotic Landscape by Henri Rousseau (1844-1910).

Perhaps this painting will give you ideas for things to put in your collage.

- Paste a strip of blue fabric right across the top of your paper. This is your sky.
- Cover the rest of the paper with a piece of green fabric. This is your background.
- Cut out lots of different sizes and shapes of leaves and trees. Do the same to make brightly colored flowers.
- Lay them on your background and overlap them. Do not glue them down yet. Rain forests have many different plants. Put the smaller leaves and trees at the top first and work down. Move them around until they look right.
- Now glue down a few shapes at a time. Start at the top and work to the bottom. Don't forget the birds and animals.

You will need:

Different types and colors of fabric, especially lots of different greens

Pictures of rain forests and jungles

Your collage box

Scissors

Glue

Cardboard or thick paper

Butterfly wings

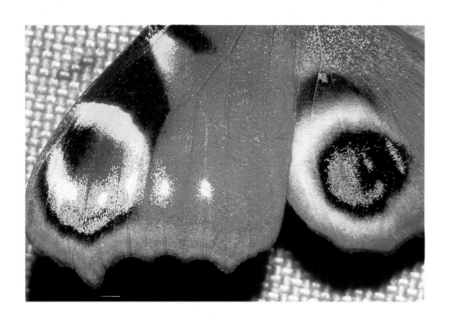

Look at this photograph. Can you guess what it is?

It is a close-up of a butterfly wing. Look at the patterns. Can you make a picture like that?

This collage is also about butterflies. The artist has used cut-out paper.

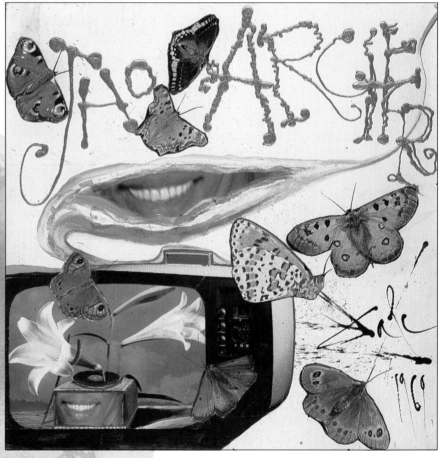

Marquette de Converture de Disque 1969
by Salvador Dali (1904 - 1989).

You will need:

Paints

Paper

Brush

Water jar

Palettes or plastic plates

Colored cellophane and
  tissue

Scissors

Glue

Cardboard

- Paint some water over a piece of paper.
- Mix some thin paint and brush a small circle of it on the wet paper.
- Mix a different, bright color and drop a little of it into the middle of the damp circle. See how the colors run. Let them dry. Try different colored circles. You can use these to help make your collage.
- Cut a small square of cardboard into a six-inch square.
- Make the background for your close-up of a butterfly wing using cellophane, tissue, and anything else you want.
- Cut or tear out the circles you have painted. Glue these onto the background.

Next time, make a whole butterfly. Hang it from the ceiling with a piece of string.

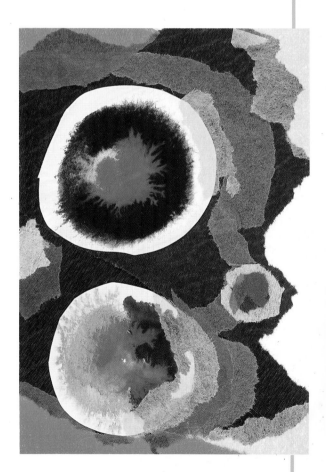

Mosaics

This is a picture of a Roman mosaic made about 1,700 years ago. Small pieces of colored stone were laid in a pattern on floors and walls. Have you ever seen a mosaic floor?

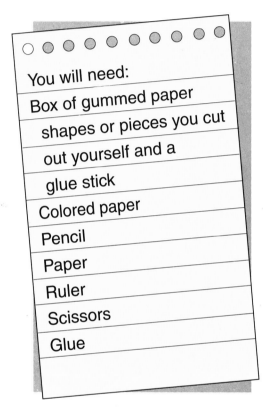

You will need:

Box of gummed paper
shapes or pieces you cut
out yourself and a
glue stick
Colored paper
Pencil
Paper
Ruler
Scissors
Glue

Box Pattern reproduced by kind permission of Bignor Roman Villa, Pulborough, West Sussex, England.

- Practice drawing some patterns.
- Make your lines straight using the ruler.
- Make triangles, squares, and rectangles.
- Choose your favorite patterns and draw them again carefully to make a picture.
- Use the gummed paper shapes to fill in your pattern.
- Cut and paste paper from bigger sheets too. Make your mosaic colorful.

You could make a long, thin mosaic border and use it to make a frame for another collage or painting.

Look at this picture of vegetables, flowers, and seed pods. See the interesting patterns they make.

- You can make a collage of the shapes and patterns that you find in fruits and vegetables, such as oranges, tomatoes, and red peppers. Ask an adult to cut one in half.
- Draw the outlines of the patterns on your paper.

· Now you are ready to make your collage.

28

- Spread thin some glue onto a small part of your drawing.
- Stick pasta and beans on it, following the lines of the pattern.
- Continue sticking down the pasta and beans, filling in your drawing until your collage is finished.

Helpful hints

You can make a beautiful collage out of just about anything, from precious gems to bottle caps. It doesn't take expensive materials to make a collage—it takes a great imagination. Use your imagination when you decide what to make and how you'll do it. Let the techniques in this book give you ideas for your own techniques. Let collages in museums, pictures in books, and everyday scenes inspire you. If you practice making collages and trust your imagination, there's no telling what kind of art you'll create!

Here are some helpful hints:

- An old fishing tackle box makes a good place to store collage materials.

- Brown parcel paper that is sold in rolls makes a good background for big collages.

- Cardboard from old cartons makes a firm backing for a collage. Stores often have old cartons that they will give away.

- Look through a kaleidoscope to get ideas for collages.

- See if you can make a collage out of unusual "theme" items, such as things you find when you're taking a walk or things that are green.

- Set up a gallery on your bedroom wall. You can put your collages in inexpensive plastic frames, tack them all to a bulletin board, or use nonstick adhesive to hang them on the wall.

- Ask a friend to make collages with you.

Glossary

Bird's-eye view Seen from above, as if by a bird.

Close-up A very close view of something.

Collage A picture made by sticking down different materials onto a background.

Corrugated cardboard A type of cardboard with ridges and grooves.

Frame A border around a picture, window, or other item.

Mold A container into which a soft material is poured and left to harden so it becomes the same shape as the mold.

Mosaic A decoration made with small pieces of colored material – often ceramic tile – that form a picture or pattern.

Overlap Laying part of one thing over part of another.

Pattern Shapes and colors that are repeated.

Pods The cases that hold the seeds of some plants, such as peas.

Pulp In this book, a soft, wet mass made by mashing paper with water.

Stained glass Colored glass.

Synagogue A Jewish place of worship.

Techniques Ways of doing something. In this book, they are different ways of making collages.

Texture The feel or look of a surface.

Theme A subject.

Further reading

Corwin, Judith Hoffman. *Papercrafts.* Crafts Around the World. New York: Franklin Watts, 1988.

Devonshire, Hillary. *Collage.* Fresh Start. New York: Franklin Watts, 1988.

Hodge, Anthony. *Collage.* Hands On Arts and Crafts. New York: Gloucester Press, 1992.

Tofts, Hannah. *The Collage Book.* Color Crafts. New York: Simon & Schuster Books for Young Readers, 1991.

Index

Acknowledgments

The publishers wish to thank the following for the use of photographs:

Bridgeman Art Library, London for David Hockney's *Le Plongeur (Paper Pool 18) 1978, 72 x 171"* Colored Pressed Paper Pulp (12 panels);

Visual Arts Library for Giuseppe Arcimboldo's *Spring*; Marc Chagall's *The Twelve Tribes of Israel, Benjamin* © ADAGP, Paris, and DACS, London 1994; Salvador Dali's *Marquette de Converture de Disque 1969* © DEMART PRO ARTE BV/DACS 1994; and Henri Rousseau's *Exotic Landscape* 1910;

The Tate Gallery (London) for Peter Blake's *The Toy Shop*;

The Tate Gallery (St. Ives) for Patrick Heron's *Design for Big Window - Tate Gallery St. Ives: April 1992*.

Additional photographs courtesy of Chris Fairclough Colour Library.

The publishers also wish to thank our models – Kerry, Anna, Manlai, and Jeremy, and our young artists Sue and Rebecca.